AN IRISH PILGRIM

D0928293

PETER BEDRICK BOOKS
New York

Contents

Introduction

This book tells the story of Finbar, a boy who lived near Bangor in the north of Ireland round about AD 600. His father was a local chieftain and a rather fierce man, but Finbar was learning to become a monk.

In this story, Finbar goes on a pilgrimage with two of the senior monks from the monastery at Bangor. After a dangerous sea crossing, they land on the coast of France and set off on their journey through hostile territory.

The aim of their pilgrimage is to follow the footsteps of Columbanus, one of the brothers from their monastery. Columbanus set off for Italy several years ago, planning to preach and teach on his way. Strange stories and reports of wonders and miracles performed by Columbanus have reached the monastery, but nobody knows where he is, or even whether he is still alive.

At the time of this story, a time often called the 'Dark Ages' by historians, France and other countries in Europe were occupied by tribes of Germanic barbarians who fought among themselves and sometimes attacked travellers passing through their lands. Many people in these tribes did not believe in Christianity, and were threatening its very existence. Scholars from the monasteries in Ireland began to journey through England and the Continent, hoping to bring back the light of Latin culture and Christianity. Columbanus was one of these monks. Other monks, like Finbar and his companions, wrote books about Columbanus and other saintly monks, which survive for us to read today.

This book tells the story of an exciting journey across France, made by a young boy and some Irish monks. At the end of the book, you can see some detailed pictures of the buildings and beautiful items the monks used in their daily lives in Ireland.

The Homecoming

Finbar shaded his eyes against the slanting sunlight. As he looked across the rampart, he could see his family and their workmen busy with their evening tasks around the fort. It was like a separate little world on its own, safely hidden behind the high bank of the rampart which surrounded it. They had all they needed there – a long hall to eat and sleep in, a barn, a pigsty, a mill for corn and a kiln for pottery. There were plows and harrows, and horses and oxen to pull them. There were cattle to provide milk and meat, and chickens and bees to give them eggs and honey.

Finbar's family had lived here for generations. All the people living in the countryside round about were under his family's protection and owed loyalty to his father. His family had workmen, called serfs, who lived in the hill fort with them and worked for them, helping to look after the animals, to grow crops or to make and

repair the buildings and equipment inside the fort. His father was a proud and important man. He obeyed only the High King himself.

It was a long time since Finbar had seen his family. Over three years ago, he had left home to live and work with the monks in the monastery at Bangor. Soon, he was going to set off on a pilgrimage, following the steps of Columbanus, one of the brothers from the monastery. It might be years before he saw his homeland and family again. What if he never returned? He knew that the journey would be dangerous. He shivered. Was it the cool evening air or was he scared?

Finbar shook himself. No, he wouldn't be frightened of the adventure ahead of him. Even if he was training to be a monk, he was still a chieftain's son!

Just then, a sudden shout made him turn and look towards the door of the long hall. His mother had seen him and was running towards him, smiling and waving. It was good to be home, even if just for a little while.

Return to Bangor

A few days later, Finbar said goodbye to his family. It was time to return to the monastery. Finbar's father travelled part of the way with him. He was on his way to an assembly, where the important men of the neighborhood discussed local politics, and hunted and feasted together.

Finbar gritted his teeth at the squeaking noise made by the wheels of his father's chariot. He knew better than to complain. His father was an important man and wanted the country people to notice his chariot approaching. He became angry if any of his serving men tried to grease its wheels.

'That may make the chariot run more smoothly,' he said, 'but it stops the noise. We can't have that! I have my honor to think of!'

Finbar thought of the times in the past when he had been to assemblies with his father. He remembered the hunts, and the feasts of wild boar and deer which had followed. They had eaten rich cream, curds, and wild berries. And, of course,

they had drunk plenty of mead and beer. While they feasted, harpists had recited poems and songs telling of the great battles and victories of the High King and his ancestors. Now that way of life was over for him. He was going to be a monk. He was going to learn to read and write holy books, sing hymns, and preach and pray.

At the crossroads, he got down from the chariot and set off on foot towards the monastery at Bangor. In the distance, he could see the monks' church, perched high above the sandy coastline.

In many ways, life at the monastery was similar to life at home. There were crops to grow and animals to be looked after. But here, there were no serfs or servants. The monks did all the work themselves. Also, Finbar, like the other boys, had to attend lessons, too. He enjoyed hearing the stories about the lives of the saints, and studying passages from the Bible. But, really, he preferred action. He was looking forward to setting off on the pilgrimage. Even the thought of the dangerous journey did not frighten him now.

Preparations

Down by the shore, everyone was very busy. The new boat would soon be ready. Finbar watched the monks hard at work. They were skilled boat builders. Already, the frame of the boat had been made from strong planks cut from ash trees. The gunwales, which formed the top rim of the boat, had been made of tough oak. Now, the boat builders were filling in the spaces between the main timbers with a latticework of smaller pieces of wood. These were nailed together, then bound criss-cross with leather thongs. Later they would be coated with the grease from sheep's wool, to protect them from rotting in the sea. Finally, the whole hull would be covered in thick ox-hide. Then it would all be given several more coats of grease to help make it waterproof.

Finbar was watching one of the monks, who was stirring a pot of melted grease.

'When I've finished this job,' said the monk, 'I'll be helping the others make a strong mast for your boat from that tree trunk. Then I'll make some oars to help you on your way when there's no wind. You've a great journey in front of you, my lad! I'll be praying with all the other monks, for God to look down from His Heaven and keep you safe!'

Finbar was going on the pilgrimage to help two of the most senior monks, Lua and Dermot. Lua, a great scholar, was strict and stern. Finbar was rather frightened of him. But he was very fond of Dermot, the other monk. Dermot was strong and brave and enjoyed a joke.

Inside the monastery, there were other preparations for the journey. The travellers were given new leather satchels, made by the monks, to carry the dry bread which would be their emergency rations. The Abbot gave them all new tunics to keep them warm and, in addition, he gave each monk a fresh tonsure. This special haircut, which left the head bare from ear to ear, would tell the world that these were not ordinary men, but monks from Ireland!

The Journey begins

They set sail early one morning, with cries of 'God speed' from the other monks ringing in their ears. The sea crossing to France was rough and stormy, and Finbar felt very sick. He was glad when they reached the safe harbor of Wissant, on the northern coast of France. As soon as they reached dry land, they all knelt down to pray.

'God has preserved us so far,' said Lua after their prayers. 'Now we must ask for His protection throughout our pilgrimage here in France. We have an important mission to accomplish. We must try to find out whether our holy brother Columbanus is still alive, and what he has been doing since he left our monastery all those years ago. We must collect all the information we can about Columbanus and write it down, so that other people may hear of his saintly life and works.

'But first of all, we must find somewhere to rest for a few hours. Perhaps there is an inn near by. Let's set off in that direction!'

They walked inland for a couple of miles, following a rough track that led up from the beach. Soon they came to an inn. It was a large building, standing at a crossroads, rather tumbledown, and with great cracks in the stonework. Finbar was surprised to see that some of the statues, which had once decorated it, had fallen off and now lay shattered on the ground.

'It was built by the Romans, hundreds of years ago,' explained Lua. 'Now that they have gone, no one has the skills or the money to repair these old buildings.' He shook his head sadly.

Outside the inn, they got talking to two other travellers, a wine merchant and a wealthy landowner. Both of the men looked doubtful when they heard of the pilgrims' plans to follow in Columbanus' footsteps.

'The roads are very dangerous,' they warned. 'There is war among our new rulers, the Franks. They don't follow the old Roman ways. The sword is their law, so keep out of their way!'

13

Attacked by Franks!

The next day, the pilgrims set out, travelling on foot along the old Roman roads. Like the inn, these were in a bad state of repair, and Finbar and his companions were soon splashed with mud from the ruts and potholes along the way.

Before long, they came to a town. They had never seen a large number of buildings clustered together around a market square before. There were no towns in Ireland; everyone there lived in isolated farms or forts. Even the monasteries were built in wild and lonely places. They gazed around in astonishment at the fine stone houses, the stately public buildings and the neatly-paved streets. But the town seemed to be deserted.

'Where are all the people?' asked Finbar.

They all jumped when a voice called out from an empty-looking house. A nervous-looking man opened the door a fraction, and gave a sigh of relief when he saw their monks' clothes.

He smiled, and greeted them in some sort of Latin. He stumbled over the words, as if he had half-forgotten the language, but the monks were just about able to understand what he was saying.

'Welcome, brothers!' he said. 'It's good to see a fellow Christian in our streets. But do take care! Those heathen Franks are on the warpath again and they've no love of monks, so keep to the shadows as much as you can!'

'We will take care, brother,' said Lua, 'but we have God's work to do and no Frankish nobleman is going to stop us!'

But he spoke too soon. As they rounded a bend in the road, a dazzling sight met their eyes. Spears, axes, swords and polished shields glittered in the sunlight. A raiding party of Franks was riding straight towards them. They were richly dressed and even their horses were decorated with jewelry made from enamels, shiny metals and glass. The monks stood in the road as if frozen, but still the riders did not stop.

'Look out!' yelled Dermot at last. 'Jump for it!'

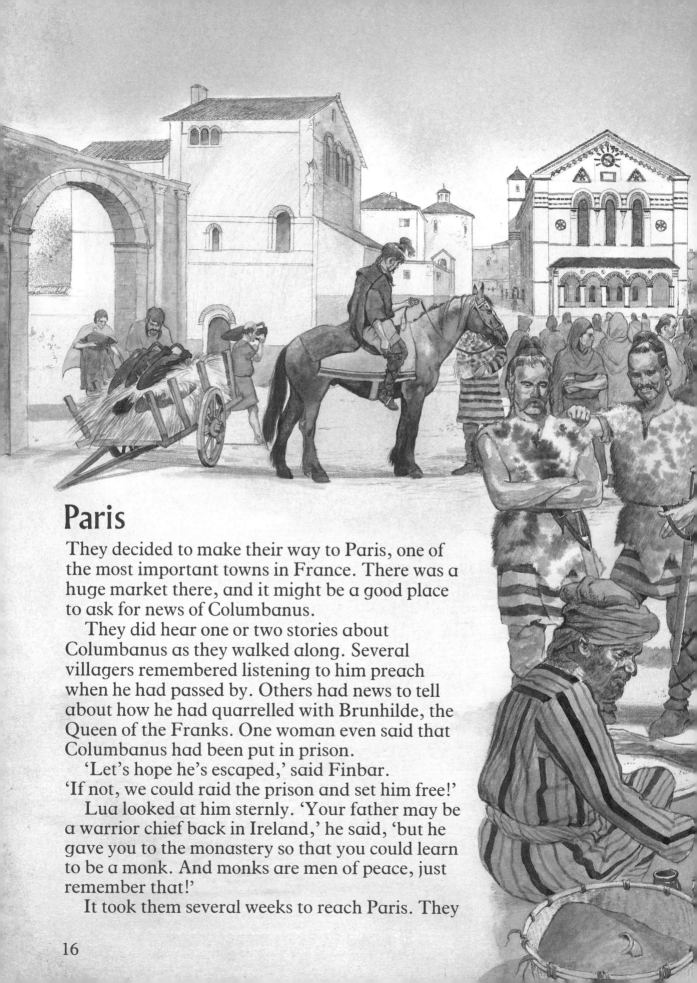

Paris

They decided to make their way to Paris, one of
the most important towns in France. There was a
huge market there, and it might be a good place
to ask for news of Columbanus.

They did hear one or two stories about
Columbanus as they walked along. Several
villagers remembered listening to him preach
when he had passed by. Others had news to tell
about how he had quarrelled with Brunhilde, the
Queen of the Franks. One woman even said that
Columbanus had been put in prison.

'Let's hope he's escaped,' said Finbar.
'If not, we could raid the prison and set him free!'

Lua looked at him sternly. 'Your father may be
a warrior chief back in Ireland,' he said, 'but he
gave you to the monastery so that you could learn
to be a monk. And monks are men of peace, just
remember that!'

It took them several weeks to reach Paris. They

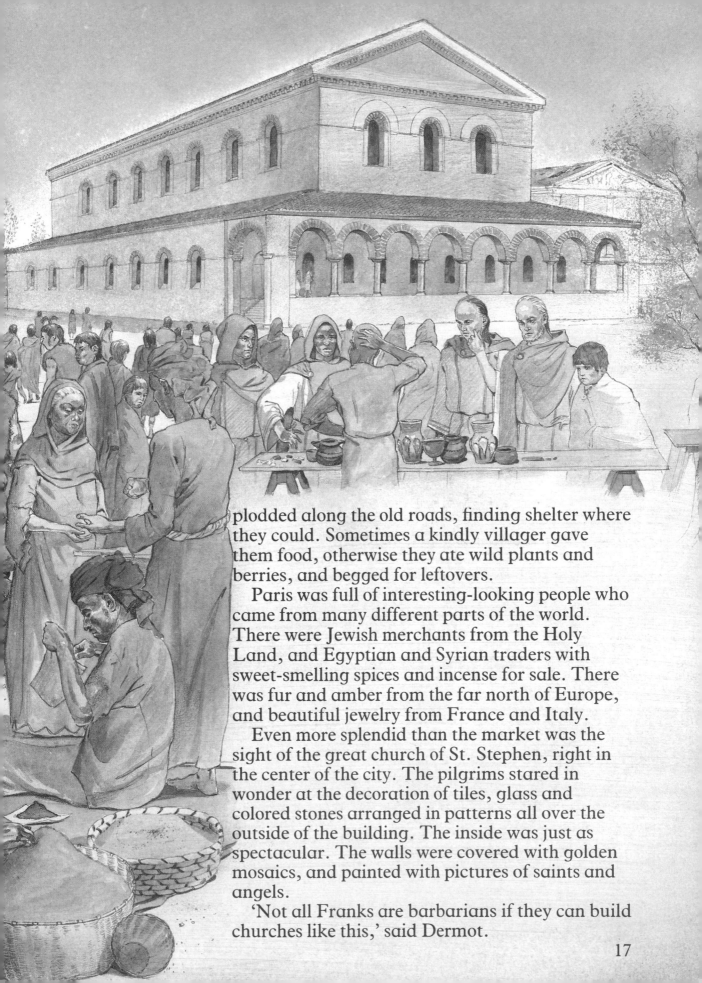

plodded along the old roads, finding shelter where they could. Sometimes a kindly villager gave them food, otherwise they ate wild plants and berries, and begged for leftovers.

Paris was full of interesting-looking people who came from many different parts of the world. There were Jewish merchants from the Holy Land, and Egyptian and Syrian traders with sweet-smelling spices and incense for sale. There was fur and amber from the far north of Europe, and beautiful jewelry from France and Italy.

Even more splendid than the market was the sight of the great church of St. Stephen, right in the center of the city. The pilgrims stared in wonder at the decoration of tiles, glass and colored stones arranged in patterns all over the outside of the building. The inside was just as spectacular. The walls were covered with golden mosaics, and painted with pictures of saints and angels.

'Not all Franks are barbarians if they can build churches like this,' said Dermot.

17

Columbanus and the Queen

They set off south-westwards from Paris. Soon, they met an old man, travelling in the same direction. They began talking as they walked along.

'So you're from Ireland,' the old man said, 'like the famous abbot at the monastery at Luxeuil.'

'Who do you mean?' asked Dermot excitedly.

'Why Father Columbanus, of course!' replied the old man. 'He was a holy man, but always quarrelling with the Queen. Let's rest a moment and I'll tell you all about it.'

Finbar sat next to the old man as he told them his story.

'One day, the Queen asked Columbanus to come and bless the marriage of her grandson, Theuderich, to a Spanish princess. Columbanus agreed; he was pleased that the Queen wanted to have God's blessing, you see. But, shortly after the wedding, the Queen took a violent dislike to her grandson's new wife, and sent her back to Spain. Her father, greatly insulted, declared war on Queen Brunhilde, and many innocent people were killed in the fighting that followed.

'When Columbanus heard of this, he was very angry and demanded to see the Queen.

'Queen Brunhilde stormed out of the palace, scowling, followed by servants carrying food and drink. "Now what's all this about, Columbanus?" she shouted. "Stop making such a dreadful fuss about nothing!"

'Columbanus looked stern. "Do you call breaking God's holy laws of marriage, and causing war and suffering to innocent people *nothing*?" he said. "You must ask forgiveness for your sins, even though you are a queen."

'Brunhilde laughed. "What, me! Say I'm sorry! Come, Columbanus, you're tired after your journey. Sit down, eat, and have a drink to refresh yourself."'

The old man continued his story. 'No one knows quite what happened next, but all the goblets of wine and plates of food crashed to the ground. Columbanus strode off without a word. I think it was a miracle,' the old man added, 'a sign that Columbanus is a messenger from God.'

The Monastery at Luxeuil

They left the old man at an inn. It had been marvellous to hear about Columbanus, but they did not know where he had gone after the miracle at Queen Brunhilde's palace.

Finbar overheard the two older monks talking.

'Well, brother,' said Dermot. 'We're not much wiser now than before we met that old chap.' His usually cheerful face looked tired and miserable. 'So far, we've met some people who think Columbanus is dead, others who think he's in prison, and still others who just don't know. The trail has gone cold!'

'Don't give up hope, my friend,' replied Lua. 'God will lead us to Columbanus, if it is His will. We'll go to the monastery at Luxeuil and see what the monks there can tell us about him.'

It was an exhausting journey. They had to trek through a lonely area of forests and high hills. All they could find to eat were roots, herbs and the bark of trees. Finbar began to wish he was back in Ireland.

They reached the monastery at last. As they feared, Columbanus was not there. The Abbot gave them a meal of peas, beans and bread, and told them how Columbanus had first come to the district in search of peace and solitude. He had found a tumbledown Roman temple to the goddess Diana at a little village called Annegray, about a day's walk from Luxeuil. He had rebuilt the temple and used it for his own prayers. Soon, other men joined him and the monastery grew. People came from miles around to join the monks at their prayers, and stories of miraculous cures performed by Columbanus spread through the countryside. Later, children were sent to the monastery to learn to read and write. Even a few proud Frankish nobles came to listen to Columbanus' preaching. The monks built a second monastery at Luxeuil itself, and then a third, at a nearby village called Fontaines.

'It was a blessed time,' said the Abbot.

A Miracle in Prison

The Abbot continued with his story. Finbar was listening to every word.

'Queen Brunhilde's grandson, Theuderich, was jealous of Columbanus' power over the local people. So, one day, Theuderich and a gang of men rode into the monastery, disturbing its holy peace with their shouts and vile swearing. But Columbanus wasn't scared. He was marvellous. I can remember the scene as if it were yesterday! He marched across to Theuderich, caught hold of his horse's bridle, and told him that he would be damned in hell for all eternity unless he gave up his evil ways and asked for God's forgiveness. Theuderich was furious and ordered his soldiers to take Columbanus off to a grim fortress near by.

'There were many prisoners inside that terrible fortress and Columbanus did what he could to

help them. One day, he spent many hours comforting a group of prisoners, whom Theuderich had unjustly condemned to die. Columbanus said some prayers and then took hold of the prisoners' heavy iron chains. They snapped as if they'd been made of grass! The prisoners escaped and fled to the nearby church, but its doors were locked and the men were trapped outside. Theuderich's soldiers, armed with lethal spears, were fast approaching, but Columbanus hurried to the men's rescue. He made the sign of the cross and at once the doors of the church flew open. The prisoners ran into the church and claimed sanctuary.'

The Abbot sighed. 'After that, Columbanus, together with many of the other monks from the monastery, was marched across country under armed guard, until they reached the port of Nevers. There, they were crowded onto a boat and taken down the river, out into the open sea. But before long the most amazing thing happened. The ship was blown to the shore and ran aground. The frightened guards freed the monks, who immediately set out for Italy.'

23

Help in the Mountains

'We'll never find Columbanus now!' said Finbar.

'Don't lose your faith, my son,' replied Lua. 'We will make our way to Rome. We have heard how Columbanus has worked many miracles. Perhaps, by another miracle, we may yet meet him ourselves!'

Their journey was getting more and more difficult. They were climbing up into high mountains. It was cold, with clammy mists and showers of sleet and snow. The people they met were unfriendly. They belonged to the Alamannian tribe and kept fiercely to their old religion. They hated the monks and the Christian religion they brought with them.

One morning, a shrill whistle sounded through the mist, and a handful of pebbles bounced on the ground just in front of them. Finbar was alarmed. Was this an ambush? Even Lua looked relieved when a boy of about Finbar's age crept out from behind a pine tree. He beckoned to them and they went across to speak to him.

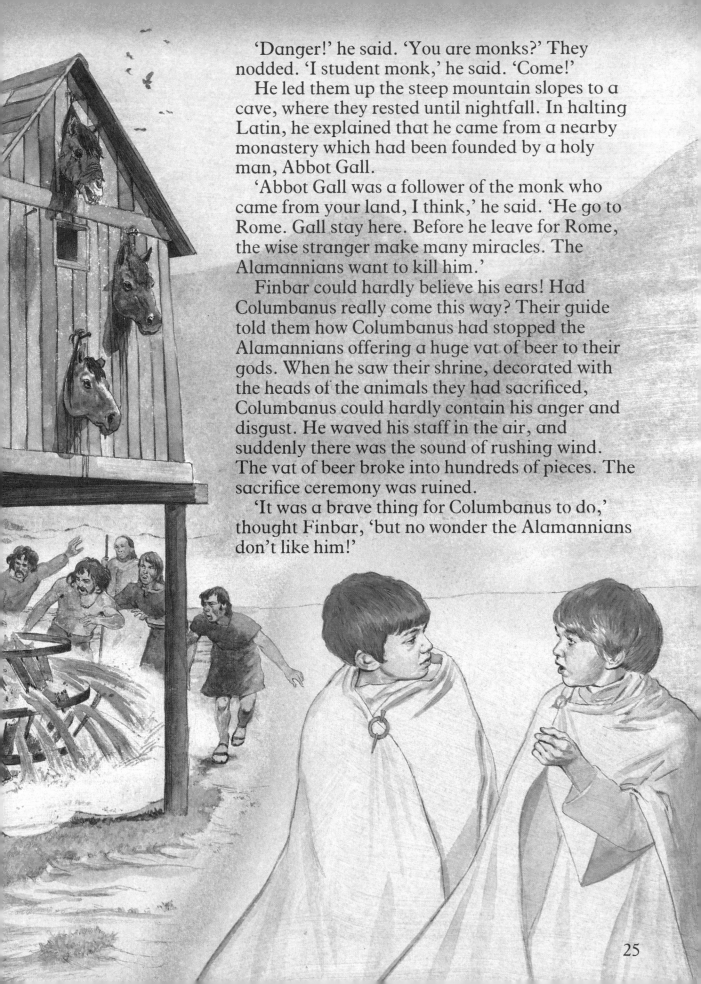

'Danger!' he said. 'You are monks?' They nodded. 'I student monk,' he said. 'Come!'

He led them up the steep mountain slopes to a cave, where they rested until nightfall. In halting Latin, he explained that he came from a nearby monastery which had been founded by a holy man, Abbot Gall.

'Abbot Gall was a follower of the monk who came from your land, I think,' he said. 'He go to Rome. Gall stay here. Before he leave for Rome, the wise stranger make many miracles. The Alamannians want to kill him.'

Finbar could hardly believe his ears! Had Columbanus really come this way? Their guide told them how Columbanus had stopped the Alamannians offering a huge vat of beer to their gods. When he saw their shrine, decorated with the heads of the animals they had sacrificed, Columbanus could hardly contain his anger and disgust. He waved his staff in the air, and suddenly there was the sound of rushing wind. The vat of beer broke into hundreds of pieces. The sacrifice ceremony was ruined.

'It was a brave thing for Columbanus to do,' thought Finbar, 'but no wonder the Alamannians don't like him!'

Journey's End

Their young guide led them through the mountain passes to the safety of Abbot Gall's monastery. It was a relief to shelter behind its strong walls, and to be greeted by the friendly, smiling monks. They rested there for several weeks, sharing the monks' simple food and joining in their prayers. Here at last, Finbar felt they were getting close to Columbanus. Abbot Gall himself told them many stories about his travels with Columbanus, and about Columbanus' strange parting words when he had left for Rome. 'He told me that I was not to celebrate the service of Mass until I knew that he was dead,' Gall said. 'I don't know why, but he was a wise and holy man and so I have obeyed him. He was an old man when he set off for Rome, and not very strong, but I hope that he managed to get to his destination in the end. The last I heard of him, he had set up another monastery at Bobbio, in Italy.'

It was not many days later that the monks were called to the monastery church. Abbot Gall was looking solemn.

'Brothers,' he said. 'Last night God sent me a message in a dream. Our brother Columbanus has gone to join the saints in Heaven. May God grant him rest.'

Finbar gasped. He felt his eyes fill with tears. But Abbot Gall went on.

'Before he died, Columbanus left his staff to our monastery. We will treasure it as a precious relic of a holy man. We are most fortunate, too, in having our Irish brothers staying with us at this time. They have agreed to go to Columbanus' tomb, collect the staff, and bring it back to us, before continuing on their way to Rome. We wish them God speed on their journey!'

Finbar looked up at Lua. The older monk, usually so severe, was smiling at him.

'God is good,' Lua said. 'Our efforts have been rewarded, and our journey's end is near. Even if we cannot speak to him in this life, we have found Columbanus at last!'

Picture Glossary

At the time of this story, round about AD 600, Europe was a dangerous place. The old Roman Empire had collapsed and warlike tribes fought among themselves for control of the land.

Ireland, which had become Christian during the Roman occupation of neighbouring Britain, had escaped all these invasions and developed strong Christian traditions.

When Irish monks like Columbanus set off on pilgrimage towards Rome, they had to travel through dangerous and hostile territory.

Houses and churches

The first churches were built with strong wooden posts and planks and a tough thatch of rushes for the roof. Later on, church buildings were made of stone. Sometimes a tower or extra room was added. Remains of these stone churches can still be seen today in many parts of Ireland.

Below: Boatbuilding

A Sideways view.
B How a boat was built: the wooden framework was covered by cross ribs laced together. These were then covered by pieces of leather, and coated with grease.
C Detail of cross ribs.

Reconstruction of a typical wooden church.

An early church, built of stone.

Saints and scholars

The church in Ireland in the 7th, 8th and 9th centuries produced many remarkable men. Some were famous for their holy lives and religious teachings; others were famous for their learning and skill as writers and artists.

These 'saints and scholars' lived together in monasteries, but also travelled widely.

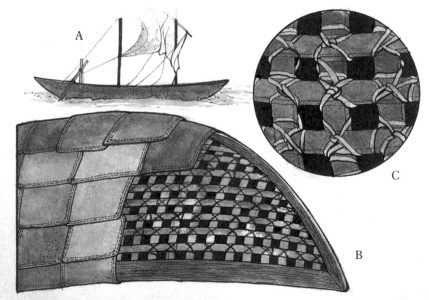

A

B

C

h[ISTORANUELA]

ʒelisuuumusⱺ echuoꝺeanꝺ

ꝺiscipulisⱺi quiuirʒo eleauis aꝺó eſt quem

Manuscripts, carvings, silverware and jewelry

1 Richly-decorated initial letter and text from the Book of Kells, produced for the Church.
2 Carved stone cross from Castledermot.
3 Silver chalice, from Ardagh, used in church.
4 Jeweled brooch, found at Tara. Perhaps worn by a chieftain.
5 Carved ivory buckle.
6 Jeweled ivory comb.
5 & 6 both from France.

Right: This map shows the earliest Irish monasteries, dating from the 5th century AD. It also shows centers of learning in Europe.

Some monks went on pilgrimages to preach and teach. This map shows some of the monasteries they founded on their travels, and also other monasteries influenced by their teachings.

Iona
Bangor
Armagh
Lindisfarne
Annegray
Luxeuil
Fontaines
Bobbio

● Irish monasteries
▲ Centers of learning.
▭ Columbanus' journeys.
● Monasteries founded by Columbanus.
● Monasteries influenced by Irish Church.